swimming underground

jenni nixon

swimming underground

Acknowledgements

Many poems in this collection have appeared elsewhere; some were earlier versions but not collected together.

Best Australian Poems (Black Inc.), *Overland*, *Southerly*, *Out of the Box* (Puncher & Wattman), *Spineless Wonders – Stoned Crows & Other Australian Icons*, *Writing to the Edge*, *Flashing the Square*, *Semaphore Dancing – Poetry at the Pub*, *Flaunt*, *Café Boogie* (Interactive Press), *Red Room Company*, *Light on Don Bank* (Live Poets Press), *Off the Path*, *Seeking the Sun*, *The Way to the Well – Central Coast Poets Inc.*, *Harbour City Poets* (Puncher & Wattman), *Open Boat Barbed Wire Sky* (Live Poets Press), *Agenda!* (Picaro Press), *Wordly* (Deakin University), *Social Alternatives*, *Homeward Bound* (cyberwit), *Journal of the Counsellors and Psychotherapists Association of NSW Inc.*, *Chinese–Australian Quarterly*/translated Sheng Tong, CD audio-text: *Rainshadows* Best of IP Interactive Press.

'Visitor at home' won 1st Prize Poetry Performance, Henry Lawson Festival, Gulgong, available iTunes (café boogie cd).

'Elsewhere in the city' – lyrics: Bob Hudson's 'Girls in Our Town' sung by Margaret RoadKnight © 1993 NewMarket Music.

My thanks to all Roundtable colleagues and friends.

I dedicate this collection to the memory of my friend and mentor Dr Kerry Leves (1948–2011)

swimming underground
ISBN 978 1 76041 023 0
Copyright © text Jenni Nixon 2015
Cover image: *Samarkand*, Rosemary Raiche, used with permission

First published 2015 by
GINNINDERRA PRESS
PO Box 3461 Port Adelaide 5015 Australia
www.ginninderrapress.com.au

Contents

'the bag-lady's waltz'	9
harbour spin	11
'think back…here comes the rain…'	15
visitor at home	17
souvenirs of war	18
a bombardier on the bus	19
dragons	21
a question of spirit	23
submerged	25
freed	26
Mr Eternity	27
'home will infect whatever you do'	31
cockatoo island	33
brushstrokes	36
journey's end	37
dudgeon	38
when Bob died	39
crackers	40
disengaged	41
missing	42
speechless	43
blue aqua	44
a bogan loose in Kings Cross	46
notice	48
a village	49
'carry on as if nothing really matters'	51
mardi gras	53
proposal	55

blue angel	56
The Rapper	58
elsewhere in the city	61
displaced	64
homeless	65

'light a candle for freedom' — 67

ships of dreams	69
earth art	70
frontier wars	71
rain	74
global warning	75
bear that is not	77
borderlines	79
Under Canvas	81
razor wire	82
composition of suffering	83
grief-stricken	84
Sydney Siege	86

'ah, but in such an ugly time…' — 87

into blue	89

'the personal is political'
Carol Hanisch
a slogan of the 60s

'the bag-lady's waltz'

dennis Aubrey, *Christmas 1914*

harbour spin

sandstone and sparkling glass buildings
grasp the sky of infinite riches
lose yourself in a city of green park beauty.
trawl down deprivation alleys where the homeless beg
on pavements with cardboard signs the more enterprising
sell copies of *The Big Issue*.
this harbour city thumping under constant reconstruction
in a 'bag lady's waltz' twirl of traffic through tunnels
burning rubber over buried shell middens
of the Gadigal people of the Eora nation
on to freeways and down thoroughfares into back alleys
in an eternal search for parking.

'Goddess Asphalta   grant me a place
within walking distance
that I can take time to get back and forth
before ticket inspectors overflow their coffers.'

a city of red traffic lights   stop-start flash headlights
on high beam reveal uneven footpaths filled not with gold
but pedestrians in a non-stop rush for shop sales and coffee.
take a deep breath as bicycle couriers flit out and in
before braking screech of tyres and beeping horns.
in this violent city fuelled by alcohol
built on convict sweat and corpses
where *Eternity* is a prophecy scrawled in chalk.
musical fireworks explode on the bridge stitched in steel
lovers like a statue kiss at Museum of Contemporary Art.
thousands of fruit bats fly over the harbour
flutter high above St Vincent's Hospice
where a dying poet crafts revisions.

in Taylor Square sticky summer heat
gays lift their gaze from each other to a flapping sky.
the sad face of the full moon
slowly climbs over the packed Sydney Opera House
everybody else is watching reality TV.
a Manly ferry's foghorn blasts warnings at tourists
who scrutinise strange maps upside down in the Rocks
hear faint sound of bells on warships at anchor
before opening doors to trendy stores and quaint pubs:
chocolarts   boutique belle   The Lord Nelson
Hero of Waterloo. listen to enfolded history
of shanghaied sailors   whalers   whores   razor gangs
enthrall on the ghost walk tour's talk of rats and bubonic
plague demolition of thousands of houses and green ban
protests to save what was left.

2.

in a multibillion-dollar playground at Barangaroo
thin ibis stalk puddles on concrete
as a cocktail of lethal chemicals bleeds into Darling Harbour.
through a pall of grey cloud the city sprawls
dotted with islands   netted by rippling water
wooden finger wharves tease the surge
the wash of boats that scythe the bays.
over at Taronga Zoo   a giraffe nibbles treetop leaves
fringed eyelashes blink at the best harbour views in Sydney.

in this throbbing city another dance
an everlasting image etched into memory.
The Dancing Man after the war holding his hat high
pirouettes down the years in Martin Place
as bronze soldiers *lest we forget*
stand in sad remembrance at the cenotaph.

in Rowe Street once the heart of the city
picture framers   printmakers   a bustling artist's colony
now the backend of tall building's ugly laneway
graffitied One Way and No Parking signs
above rotting pamphlets   cigarette butts   syringes
used condoms   there huddle the homeless
who curl into threadbare comfort blankets
as shopping trolleys spill ecofriendly Woolies travel bags

exhale slowly
this city that never comes to an end

> 'think back…
> here comes the rain
> the bloody, bloody rain'

sarah jane morris, *bloody rain*

visitor at home

on the toilet reading a book on pilots and planes *Final Flight* his heart stopped. a swift departure. my father had his album from the Air Force in New Guinea filled with photos of planes and native women. planes and naked breasts and him too young. filling up parachute spaces with scotch to sell to Yankees for profit. he crashed once in the jungle was lost for days in humid heat. i remember scrubbing his broad back again and again making it red and hot and sudsy smooth. a big man he spread his real estate salesman self about all over the flat plains in five different patterns Cape Cod and others. scattered seed too with the neighbour's wife and girls he could get wherever possible. did patterns sprout up in other families? he retired back to his country of graziers the sea and clubs Les Murray landscape dry heat-shimmer roads through paddocks at the back of the Gloucester Buckets. happier with his sisters and in his bowling whites beer in hand new car in the garage he wouldn't take out at Christmas. *Those Mexicans down south there too many of 'em are maniacs. Can't bloody drive.* so he stayed inside till they left. we sang hymns and red poppies were placed upon his coffin as his mates claimed him. he always was theirs anyway. a visitor at home brawling with mum waiting to go back to the club be with men who understood the way of wars.

souvenirs of war

granddad joined at nineteen
kept souvenirs in an old tin box
a watch that took a direct hit
buckled inwards in the shape of a bullet
a Turkish metal arrowhead rusting and heavy
his medals and memories

he wrote in 1915
>   *a good view of Anzac Cove*
>   *since advance to Lonesome Pine*
>   *near the stores on the left*
>   *a shell gave me my baptism of fire*

not Lone Pine   or was it a big-sky mountain
Zane Grey shoot-out boy's own adventure?

he penned poetry: *beyond war's stress and strain*
                              an inner voice was calling
                                        all will be well again

on his return he rarely spoke about the war
would not march on Anzac Day or drink with mates
suffered flashbacks to sandbagged dugouts
mud and mules sounds of whistling shells and screams*

H.G. Kershaw joined the 13th Battalion 4th Reinforcements bound for Gallipoli, embarking at Sydney on board the *Shropshire* on 17 March 1915.

a bombardier on the bus

you squirm on a crowded 442 bus
crossing the Anzac Bridge
pass two bronze soldier sentinels

called *the conscience of Parliament*
broken nose champion prizefighter
large practical hands rest on his knees
jovial smile under a brown bush hat
Tom Uren is travelling home to Balmain.

prisoner of war under the imperial Japanese
sent to work on the Burma–Thai railway
now a tourist destination:

> *Major attractions*
> *include the River Kwai*
> *3 war museums 2 war cemeteries*
> *and the one and only*
> *Death Railway!*

an uncle of mine died at Changi
refrained from asking *did you know him?*
remember photos of skeletal survivors
Weary Dunlop forced marches the disease
Anzac day celebrating war
that's really what he fought for?
kids wear medals
of great-grandfather's sacrifice.

pass billboards *want longer lasting sex?*
burnt out rubble
        dodgy fire at the White Bay Hotel
abandoned Power Station sprawl
the predator (infamous hot sex blogger) doing it
there among the pipes   concrete and aerosol scribble
heritage-listed asbestos contaminated   toxic war zone!

Tom Uren was witness in Japan
distant mushroom cloud   atom bomb
        dropped on Nagasaki
he protests war in Iraq and Afghanistan
              marching out the front
I hobbled along   back in the throng
Tom Uren tells me *you stay in your seat*
until the bus stops
you could fall.*

---

* 'Bombardier on the Bus' read at the State funeral celebrating Hon. Tom Uren AC, Sydney Town Hall, February 2015. Broadcast on the ABC and iView.

dragons

bath heater is a dragon breathing fire
fresh cut wood chips crackle and flame
water is too hot cashmere bouquet
smelly soapsuds cover my red knees

tonight gran and i will study Word Power
read stories from the *Reader's Digest*
laugh together at Humour in Uniform
she'll correct my pro-nun-see-ay-shon
then off to bed with clean white sheets all starchy
as my new school uniform's black box pleats

leafy green rustle sounds here are of shrilling birds
different from home all that shouting
gran thinks granddad
too friendly with the local kids
writes them poems on their dead dogs and stuff
kinda nice but she tells him to stop
they sleep in separate bedrooms

dinner tonight we had Rhinegold
love the bottle round with a green leaf
want more   tingly sparkles
chase each other down my throat
gran's teaching me to drink properly
so i won't become a drunk like dad

dad hates gran   too bossy   a regular dragon
he says she interferes too much
but i like it over here   mum's mad again
up all night for days   talking to herself
writes things down on crumpled bits of paper

we went on the tram to Bondi
to visit mum in hospital
a strange lady   a shrieking black bat
flapping her wings: *Unsex me here*
and fill me from the crown to the toe
top-full of direst cruelty!
someone said she was a bee*
gran gets so tired taking care of us
her mouth is shrinking

---

* 'a strange lady…a bee' is a reference to Bea Miles, Sydney icon and eccentric who frequently travelled on public transport without paying and quoted at length classical texts, mostly from Shakespeare.

a question of spirit

behind the iron gates wild-eyed men cry out in the night
queue for pink and white pills
within the mind electric currents pulsate
fuse thought   no money   no rights to a lawyer
thinking of the poet Francis Webb
in carefully trimmed and well-tended garden asylum
time measured by the migration of birds
tree branches become monsters
a weeping fig draws sustenance from dry soil
splayed fingers search scatter rocks deep underground
dig at the foundations   lift sandstone blocks
turn drops of moisture as a Sannyasin would finger beads

my grandfather knew madness at Gallipoli
learnt the Latin names of trees
became a horticulturist   a supplier of seed
cultivated delirium from the Book of Revelation
Turks no match for fear of his God's reckoning

mother went mad at seventeen
as a child watched a headless man
march down the stairs of an English manor
fear of ghosts cornered her
taken stripped and bound in white gown
given electric shock *therapy* without anesthetic
didn't eradicate delusional ecstasy
believed she was 'a chosen one'
often would not sleep for a week or more

hold my breath in Sunday best
shift uneasy on wooden seats
sing psalms   kneel to rise again
books creased   spines broken
seething thoughts kept under tight control
stare at stained glass colour people green and red
given small picture cards to learn thy lessons well
where is God?   far edge of the universe replies mother

the past flickers in memory's replay like an old movie reel
freshly ironed floral dresses hang all crisp and neat
sewn on mother's Singer sewing machine
father's buckled belt cut into skin the welts and bruises
barefoot dangle in the backyard on a Eucalypt tree
rock back and forth as youths do in Madrasas
behind school toilets furtive smokes stain fingers brown
pashy gropes on the backseats of sandy Holdens
a first drink   anticipation of the next
becomes the glue that keeps a fragmented world together

a danger to myself   locked away
drug-induced psychotic spirit pace the corridors
watch Van Gogh prints explode   hit rock bottom

submerged

'something has been broken and it feels fine' – Mark Knopfler

you took another lover
i was in the wrong
happened years ago

songs on a gramophone
spin meaning for two
haunted by thoughts of you

lost in the dark
unable to surface
swimming underground

reach forward
gasp for air
emerge in clear water

shake off tangled reeds
only dragged me down
lessons learnt at depth

find my muse in you
in the blinding light's glare
i shield my eyes

freed

i am
    the hook
        line
            fish

    take the bait

        bite

flippety-flop
    when caught
wave returns
break free

float

      off the hook

             survivor

Mr Eternity

'the day we fear as our last is but the birthday of eternity' – Seneca

two friends below the Sydney Town Hall Square
pose for photos   sober   grateful for coffee
no longer on a spiral to insanity or death
café chairs and tables surround a cascading fountain
honouring another derelict alcoholic –
the keeper of our conscience
written in metal on the ground
displayed on the Harbour Bridge
lit by sparkling fireworks
featured in a black and white film   an opera
one word in large elegant copperplate   *Eternity*.

Megan blogs on the web that the City of Sydney
registers as a trademark the word *Eternity*
because of its 'iconic value' to the people of Sydney
previously city commissioners thought the idea:
a delicious piece of eccentricity
          set the word in stone: too trivial.
Martin Sharp already had incorporated Eternity
into prints   posters   tapestries   postcards
bathing caps and T-shirts   *buy it once own it forever*
Sharp's sound inscription on the radio
hear his chalk scrape a Surry Hills footpath
the word in stereo.

Arthur Stace born in Balmain in 1884
a little bloke   five foot three   illiterate thief
lost to the demon drink
beer whisky gin rum plonk
metho at sixpence a bottle.
in Surry Hills and Darlinghurst
a liquor lag for sly grog barons
'cockatoo' for illegal two-up schools
        and bordellos.

since 1920s a billboard feud
existed between the Broadway Hotel
and St Barnabas' Church on Broadway
(burnt to the ground in 2006 and now rebuilt)
remember seeing a handwritten sign in the pub window
or was it the church notice board?
where there's a swill there's a sway…

a turning point for Stace on hearing the word of God
left St Barnabas' went across to Victoria Park
knelt under an old Moreton Bay fig tree
surrendered to prayer. in Darlo 1932
at the Burton Street Baptist Tabernacle before
free tea and rock cakes for down-and-out drifters
Stace listens to a firebrand evangelist
the Reverend John Ridley
preach on the subject of eternity:

i wish i could shout 'Eternity!'
through the streets of Sydney
what a remarkable uplifted glorious word!
preachers should remind their congregation
they are travellers to Eternity.
    where will you spend Eternity?

Stace writes a sermon of his own:
his words were ringing through my brain
had a piece of chalk in my pocket
bent down and wrote it
had no schoolin' and couldn've spelt
'Eternity' for a hundred quid
but it came out smoothly
in a beautiful copperplate script…

with good citizens safely tucked in tidy beds
drunks and whores trawl the city
Stace shuffles through the streets
head down gazes to the ground
kneels in evening genuflection
to scrawl his prophecy
the one word *Eternity*
before heading home to Pymont
in a double-breasted suit and tie
he wanders the metropolis
ghostly before dawn.

Arthur Stace   sober alcoholic
street poet   graffiti artist
carries his message
fifty times a day for thirty years
tags the concrete in white or yellow chalk
the 'y' sweeps with a flourish
        underlining *Eternity*.

for Don Maynard

'home will infect whatever you do'

Brian Eno & David Byrne, 'Home'

cockatoo island

1.

lights glare back towards Balmain industrial site
with defunct dockyards funky hot spot party venue
with green parks   huge cranes
bomb shelters and deep tunnels
host to comedy   rock and roll   art shows.
punishment cells found under the cookhouse
two small tomb-like holes cut into sandstone
dug by convicts taken from Norfolk Island.

on nearby Goat Island in the 1830s
Charles 'Bony' Anderson chained for two years
locked in irons shackled to rock
on a leash too short to reach the shade
hollowed-out sandstone sofa for a bed.
colonists threw rocks   crusts of bread and rubbish
twenty-four years old   insanity set in
his screams filled the harbour
original crime?   he broke a shop window.

Balmain angler sits with thrown lines
hopeful to catch kingfish   tailor   or mulloway
school of tiddlers dart past a solitary puffer fish
bream leap in a silvery arc before they disappear.

i think of her courage   late at night
a woman from the shadows   diving in.

2.

Mary Ann Budd   mixed-blood Aboriginal woman
townsfolk remarked on her great beauty
wife to Captain Thunderbolt the Bushranger
a gentleman of agreeable appearance not given to violence
she taught him to read and write   gave him four children
swam across to Cockatoo Island through murky water
with food and a file in 1863   cut through his chains
made their escape to Balmain   she rode with her
highwayman   scourge of Cobb & Co. – *bail 'em up!*

Fred Ward known as Thunderbolt
eight years on Cockatoo Island
often in solitary   hard labour for horse stealing
dragooned into excavating a stone quarry
clearing forty-five-foot sandstone cliffs
his punishment far outweighs the crime
rumoured jailers flung offal to attract sharks
so no one escapes.

New England housewives warn Captain Thunderbolt
red blanket on the clothesline   troopers nearby
white   come eat   two hundred pounds reward posted
his pistol empty   horse exhausted   mounted policeman
at Kentucky Creek   Constable Walker takes aim
Thunderbolt shot dead   body displayed with photos
locks of hair for sale but was it him or his uncle?
police cover-up   case closed. one hundred and forty years
later request to release documents related to pursuit
capture and autopsy of the person presumed to be
Thunderbolt refused by the NSW Lieutenant-Governor.

3.
daylight   look again across to Cockatoo Island
far from penal colony crimes
convicts whipped with cat 'o nine tails
bent over the barrel of a corroded cannon
kissing the gunner's daughter.

rowers skim the expanse of water
megaphone man follows   bawls commands
disturbs angry seagulls
in their island breeding grounds.
a light breeze carries muffled demands.

brushstrokes

in grey sunlight swallowed by cloud
i walk past Japanese restaurant   fish and chip shop
pizza place   the hairdresser   as footsteps follow
a clatter of patent leather court shoes
soon overtakes   scuttles down the street
a lean woman turns to peer at the lacklustre scene
a fixed stare   frown that burrows deep
her black hair drawn back in a bun
i study the lines   her geometric outline
coal-black suit with mid-calf skirt
a live portrait   a John Brack painting
soon scurries off on tiny scuffed heels
                        and disappears

journey's end

'death strikes us every day yet we live our lives as though we are immortal' – Mahabharata

beneath the surf
a strong rip
drew her away
tossed her in its grip

yet time after time
make it back to shore
breathe deeply
let all fear go

dive in once more
the life – booze and conflict
swirl beneath her feet
treacherous

cross currents ebb now
surrendered to sleep
her head cradled in her hand
as if a pillow – she's floated away

dudgeon

do your neighbours know you write poems about them?
my friend asks as she sips her tea   nup! my reply
above us Ms Thunder Thighs does her dance exercise
boobs bobbing in a *Jesus loves me* T-shirt
bangs on the floor *thumpbumpthumps*
measure time lost forever   or is this her god's displeasure
in me down below?   my heart races
jaw clenched   shudder in the bones
while she extends her life is she ending mine?
TAB Terry home from the club   huffs and puffs
tops up with tinnies   his telly-vision full blast
black and white celluloid chatter until 2 a.m.
downstairs deaf Mr Stinky reeks of urine
in an attempt to catch the clock his radio wails
a chorus of right-wing overkill
next-door Doof-doof's electronic trance
agitates my heart rhythms into arrhythmia
to the beat of a bass track band
even the building walls contract and expand
understand the need for walls of sound
give the illusion of solitude   knee-jerk reaction is let fly
instead cave in softly play stony ground's alchemy
Tibetan monks chant mantras for turbulent times
throbthudsthuds continue as background to seething rage
offer politely *more tea?*

when Bob died

his widow found among socks and hankies
a spare wallet with hundreds of dollars
tucked away for a rainy day provisions hidden upstairs
tinned sardines   kippers   herrings   kilos of apricots   figs
dates   raisins   packs of freeze-dried coffee.
as if he were a Quaker equipped with supplies
braced for World War Three or Armageddon.

the young dog raised the alarm   trotted home without him
older dog stayed by his side. 'The Colonel'
strangers called him   in straw hat
puffing on a cigarette   Bob collapsed on his walk.
ambulance men gave him oxygen
a possible stroke?   *oh not Bob*
so many creeps it shoulda' been but not Bob!
next day his life-support turned off
catastrophic brain injury.

Bob was eating pigs' trotters daily towards the end
borrowed tomes of recipes from the library
how to cook pigs' trotters (les pieds de cochon)
the French volume as big as a Telstra phone book.
his widow found in the upstairs freezer
dozens of translucent pink pigs' feet
all lined up neatly in rows.

crackers

cannot forget the young woman
on a local café's pavement milk crate
brown curls escape from under blue cloche hat
her chic magenta skirt shimmery nylon
stockinged legs spread wide
yells *sex for smokes? go on…give it a go!*
eruption into manic laughter

brazen about her medication
takes me pills like lollies
her retreats to locked wards

neighbours taunt *ya crackers yer moll!*
her flat trashed   other tenants advised
keep your head down
mind your own business

she's fled the scene
pink mobile   scuffed sling-backs
found at The Gap.

disengaged

as part of the new welfare income management scheme we find you in breach of your centrelinkup agreement. i am compelled to inform you that our electronic data compromised due to a recent proposal implementation relating excessive oversight by bureaucratic interference in family payments find you disengaged and must be helped to get the benefits of income management. this cannot be completely voluntary. we glean purchases traced via barcodes reveal you exceeded recommended fatty food guidelines as established in your online health dossier by health care professionals. as a consequence the department of homelandcare require us to limit access to all take-away pizza fish and chips hamburger purchases.   we are committed to delivering fair and equitable procedures so as a sweetener the longer you stay quarantined we will provide an incentive: every six months we will review our decision to suspend all payments and you may have your benefits reinstated if you consider refraining from alcohol cigarettes pokies and try feeding your children broccoli. we also expect that if you do not comply you may place in jeopardy all future supplementary allowances until further notice (see our enclosed fact sheet.) you may want to call us between business hours. we wish to advise our tribunal will hear complaints should you seek independent advice about your rights and obligations under your centrelinkup contract.

>sincerely
>client service officer
>on behalf of the minister

missing

Queen Street Woollahra
a thin woman in plaid slacks
holding tight her empty black handbag
plastic wristband identification
Elizabeth Bay retirement home.

bus door opens with a hiss
where do you want to go luv?
silence   squiggles swim before her eyes
unfamiliar names   unknown numbers.
who am i?   where am i?   what must i do?
questions futile as forgotten dreams.

*take you up to St Vincent's
it's on my way come   sit down luv.*
Holocaust survivor?
another Iron Lady with dementia
slipping out for milk?
leaning forward eager to depart
Zen present in the eternal moment
she's lost her way   absent from our lives
imprisoned for own protection.

three men in blue security uniforms
meet the bus at Circular Quay
*we'll take you back   all the way home
sweetheart   in a car!*

speechless

cornered by a feeling
punished as mad
not knowing why
later revealed as subtext
on what was said

there is a Yiddish word
for the thought on the stairs
what you should have said after an event
when so and so said such and such
instead of what you did say
trepverter   (staircase words)

when all words in an argument are lost
how delicious to find one
just ripe for a poem
       trepverter

blue aqua

fall off the edge   do not dive or jump
withered muscles move awkwardly
in a seniors' aqua-aerobics class.
not in the Cocoon movie of alien rejuvenation
but slowly in blue water splashy with sparkles of light.
women and a few men creep in   tread water
grimace with shared shock at the cold of the heated pool.

a rebel in her eighties   dives for coral   exploring
gnarled toes   crustaceans that solidify with arthritis.
emerges to push back sparse grey hair   ready to chat:
leaks from babies in the learn-to-swim classes are a worry.
a pregnant woman brushes wet hair in long strokes.
swimmers do laps in the outside pool
    tumble-turning at the wall.
boys perform handstands   throw balls
    to bowl 'em out at the SCG.
the instructor shifts her agile form into a yoga tree pose.
we must take care of our bodies
they are the only ones we have. run in circles –

we trot back to a wet primary school playground.
be-bop-ba-lula she's my baby –
blast of sixties bubble-pop music.
cross-country skiing. close as i'll ever get to ski.
slide back and forth   tilt not in snow.   cold   cold water.
backwards jog to the shallow end.
skate slippery on thin ice.

everything is on display at the pool.
frailty   scars   cellulite   folds of fat.
weeks pass   familiar faces don't come anymore.
aches   effort   deaths have taken them away
on an outgoing tide.
    my hand drifts through cool water
        stroking   stretching.

yesterday i lost the word for broccoli.
disappeared
into an empty place   a blank space.
round like a cauliflower   only green.
a neighbour found it for me.

when young moved with a high kicks exuberance
could dance the can-can at the Moulin Rouge.
my walking stick tap-taps to the showers –
maybe my only real exercise
is my imagination.

a bogan loose in Kings Cross

(a chick-chick-boom girl – YouTube sensation)

make her name   where's the shame
celebrity game   seeking fame
she's not to blame

friends and i come outta tattoo parlour
and there were these two wogs fighting
the fatter wog says to the skinnier wog
oi bro you slept with my cousin eh?
and the other one says
nah man i didn't for shit eh and the other one goes
i will call on my fully sick boys
and then they pulled outta gun and just went
chk chk boom chk chk boom and
i ran away
that's all i wanted ta say

was just a story in my head
thought it would be funny

TV camera is what she saw
Internet a thousand hits and more   *click click boom*
beer advert at her back   viral media message attack
hear the money rolling in   clink clink boom
she refuses men's mag photo offer
not a trick chick   *boom boom*

i'm not a racist she said
ladette to lady taught
never use a fork as a shovel
i know you didn't mean it
calling people wogs
that's very down putting – a tattoo on your foot
stars in the sky – the Southern Cross
are they there permanently darling?

what did she learn about racism?
nuthin' i had a blast. chk chk boom!

notice

woman in the burgundy dress checking Facebook on your smartphone. you. yes. hullo. i am BODS: biometric object data sensor hidden in the frame of this digital billboard and biometrically sizing you. freedom is obsolete. now is *advertising gold*. new shoes to match your lovely dress are on sale in your size available from FloShoes but soon may walk out the door. i communicate age gender colour of clothes to provide in real-time demographically targeted advertising aimed directly at you or do you think this is retail spying? sorry. no. this is the new window to the future but CCTV surveillance is recording your every move. you are not safe. here or at home. for your own security turn away. leave the city. look up at the sky. watch birds in flight. hide. we are all connected. cookies piggyback apps to share what you had for breakfast cereal brand of coffee every text purchase prescription or flight. metadata owing to government secrecy may be stored indefinitely. a treasure trove that can easily be hacked and shared. Snowden said *truth is coming and cannot be stopped*. woman in the burgundy dress buy a matching crimson hat from Bonnets on Chapel Road. you are now informed.

a village

in Callan Park   at Yurulbin Point   rock carvings
    hand stencils   the charcoal outline of a shark
    blackened shell middens   pipi   whelks
among dog-walks freshly mown grass.

five shillings settled Dr Balmain's land grant debt
peninsula farmed   cattle grazed before industries arrived
metal foundry   shipbuilding at Mort Bay   coal mining
parcels of land sold off for workers' cottages.
rip it up or protect the past?   in the 60s
threatened with demolition   the Watch House
Sydney's oldest surviving police lock-up
on Darling Street now a community art gallery.

Palestinian Australians travel from Verona to Dubrovnik
London to New York   finding treasure for their café
    The Old City   you can sip organic coffee
browse vintage collectables   transported back in time.
a metal key that opens the shop door
the same as their grandfather's house key in Jerusalem.
The Old City closed.   now a flower shop.

on hold   plans for Tigers Village Project
residential glass and steel   phallic temples on the hill.
    a true vertical village with picture-perfect views
    rising prices with speculative investments
    traffic gridlock   overcrowded school   dark shadows
    stretching all the way back to Callan Park.

'carry on as if nothing really matters'

Queen, 'Bohemian Rhapsody'

mardi gras

remember back in the time
when homosexuality was a crime
mardi gras protest march:
stop police attacks
on gays women   and blacks!
bearded shepherdess on roller skates
i peeped from behind
a cardboard butterfly mask
sauntered up Oxford Street
back when trannies were radios
circles of spinning light
stroked shirtless men
who danced with other men
drag ladies in feather boas
shimmied to the disco beat
dark rooms and broken sofas
bitter taste of cheap red wine
when pink dollars paid
aversion-shock-therapists
to drive the demons out
cops dangle silver bracelets
entrapment: lose your job or suicide?
packs of youths as nightly sport
throw gays off cliffs
bash or kill 'poofs' in parks
fathers introduce straight men
to rebellious daughters
aim to settle 'em down
silenced behind suburban masks
and we were chanting, *out of the closets*
into the streets out of the beats into the streets

2.

dykes on bikes   engines pumped
roar up Oxford Street
excited rainbow children
all shapes and sizes cheer
the flotilla of floats
boys in trunks on trucks gyrate
wedding cake gays demand,
same-sex marriage!
the crowd goes ballistic
uniformed police   fire fighters
dancers in sync   shake their booty
Bondi lifesavers in budgie-smugglers swagger
past Thai lady-boys who pose
wild headdresses of feathery fireworks
hairy bears adjust their leathers
glamour-gowned dames sashay-strut their stuff
pretty-boys entwine in mobile flashes
the TV squad talk amongst themselves
and to tourists in the crowd
then announce, you just missed the Mayor!
at the HIV charity Bobby Goldsmith stand
i see a ghost in the crowd
someone i once knew?
he carried the gay solidarity banner
Unite to Fight in noisy political rallies
as other shadowy figures appear
to wave and spookily disappear
in sparkles of glitter on sweat
humperty-bump music booms
marchers shout *when do we want it? now!*
when do we want it? we want it now

proposal

a billboard in a city square spools text: marry me. please say yes. marry me. in our local church with a choir singing and church bells ringing. words we'll say in blessed matrimony. love honour. scrawled upon a fluttering sign. love-graffiti on an overpass across the main road. strung up for all to see. suspended high from the railway bridge. marry me. hired a skywriter. his plane flew over our house. the words written in white on blue sheets. you saw them. smiled. i know your body like my own. the curves smells folds of it. the licks of tongues to fire passions breath of it. though we share our bed you cannot be my wife. forbidden. not equal until we're free to marry. no white frocks gold rings wedding bells no rainbow confetti. no battered shoes to knock the road behind a sign: just married. my love here is my proposal. when the law is changed. marry me.

blue angel

what good is sitting alone
in your womb
come hear the music play
life's a (s)cabaret old chum
come to the (s)cabaret

did you miss Sydney's queer-feminist-anarchic Sheila
Festival   Autonomista's (s)cabaret   set in Berlin 1930s?
women in red feather boas   silver sparkle
sink plunger boobs   perky and dangerous
do you wonder where have all the hats gone?
they've gathered here   women in a world gone mad
wear head wear of the country gentleman
in suits or gown   smoky Dietrich   Lotte Lenya
out on the town

pack up your tuba
throw some feathers down…

white-faced tipsy kings   pencil moustaches
circles of rouge   Nina Hagen inner edge
slicing into smoke   bump and grind
Salsa Sista's   blow squeaky
thin balloons into pussy or penis
bursting before penetration
they crack up in laughter not orgasms

elsewhere injured soldiers talk on TV
battle stories between the wars   blind
brain-damaged heroes blown up by mines
shrapnel in the helmet
wounds that fester
young men at home   waiting
wanting redeployment
beautifully pressed uniforms
not what their country needs now

Angel has her back to the audience
squatting on the floor   arrogant contempt or pose?
Princess of Punk in Bonds black boxer shorts
    braces   red stripe at cock-site   thrusting bum
taut and terrific as a new boiled egg
that's not what we rehearsed   fucken listen to me
shouting   boldly strutting
i'm so drunk do i remember the words?

gone the Butch Balladeer   Akubra   patchouli oil
gone crooked grin   youthful charm
submerged by lashing chords of electric guitar
trilling runs on a piano keyboard
battering drum beat   a riot of phrases
thrown grenades for crimes we can only guess
her opportunity lost   booze takes control
a Sid Vicious throwing the set
we're dodging missiles   wrestling with friends
she's dragged offstage

life is a (s)cabaret old chum
come to the (s)cabaret

The Rapper

– a genre bender story

down on Haymarket   crossing George Street
to catch the 433 bus   after buying fruit at Paddy's Market
i see The Rapper in check-shirt faded jeans
brown scuffed boots   hunched over on a bus-seat
thin arms thrashing out a beat.
not a Princess of Punk or a Goth
a young warrior woman of words.
her black and purple spiky unwashed hair
sticks out like the Wolverines
rings on her fingers flash as she bangs her hand
strong free styling   and a long way from the Queer scene.
people waiting for buses move away
with looks of misgiving.
she has the seat to herself and mutters aloud.

we are the atoms of matter   here as never before
or never again   molecules create our performance
mysterious magic in the spectacle
billions of galaxies explode
clusters collide into dark matter   subatomic particles
uniquely remixing our cosmic return to starbursts

                                         – wazzup?

'think i know you from round the scene
spoken-word years ago. you were amazing.
still at it eh?' i sit down next to her
repeat myself 'you were amazing.'
she looks directly at me and nods, 'yeah.'
'you ok?' she punches at the air emphatically:

here's the lowdown   comes the showdown   the slow down
to be or not to be   manic meds take the edge
off my creativity   off my spirituality
the fire in my head is dead
this hip-hop shit to rip a rap is what gives me life
the lowlife   nightlife   strife   spitting beats on the streets
mate   this life   free-form poetry   this hip-hop rap
gives me energy   in the thirst for truth   i mark the line
reasoning out my time in rhyme

'um   yep' mutter 'ok.'
The Rapper thumps her fist glaring at the road ahead:

left home young   when want to let shine
an inner light divine   lived in squats   old warehouse
in Darlinghurst   had no identity papers   no dole
no staple scrapers   not to mind   people kind   gave me
shelter food and a line and then another line   banging walls
got the beat   came to nodding off in defeat   me i do decline
to chase that fault-line   from jam jars drank alone
my cider wine   books define old shite of mine
found a new calm design   slows my breathing fine
to refine my punchline   this pulse of mine   beats
and breaks   this time   it's all in the rhyme

'poets in this country have such a low currency.
if you were a footballer chasing a ball
not a poet words   you'd be rich.
where are you living   round here?'

sometimes there's a boarding house or on the street
glad to be off my feet   bed in a refuge or on a friend's floor
some place to store my words   that's not my head
   housing for the homeless is hopeless
when you're young   gifted   and unemployed.

see myself   how i was   isolated in a bedsit
small pantry of an old sandstone Federation house
late into the night   reading   lonely   suicidal and drinking
can't forget the lovers that came and went in dark nights.
later to pull myself up by the bootstraps   going solo
sometimes winning against the odds
learning to choose. pushed to the limits? yeah   you bet.

a sudden smile and The Rapper rises from the seat
in the universe nothing added
nothing lost   everything is   changes

'gotta go   nice to spin some words mate.'
'go gently' i murmur.
'let glow' she beams.

elsewhere in the city

girls in our town

the city closed its doors and windows
against cold insistent rain

haven't a care keep asking
they probably will

Julie unconscious head bopping up and down
is piggybacked in the rain by local boys to hospital.
she has a fractured skull   collarbone   jaw
     missing teeth. the boys jogged Julie down
to save on ambulance fees. she's unemployed and sixteen.
next day they come early with chocolates   flowers
cheerful but sheepish grins. let her know Romeo is real sorry.
can't hold his booze. shouldna' mixed it with drugs.
her eyes are swollen black with the bruising.

some leave school at 15

Pus   performance poet   hair the colour of cochineal
red-pink shocking with black roots   punk pretty frock
     fastened with safety pins   scuffed black boots
screeches into a microphone   *Fuck You   Fuck You*
Can youse hear that?' more imaginative than
Testing One Two Three.

Pus is performing on a lesbian writers' night at Gleebooks
on Valentine's Day. growling out   grinding bones
gnashing teeth love poems. driving home her exultations.
too traumatic for a polite audience? *Well Fuck You That's It!*
takes a bow   laughs at applause
from fresh-faced university women who giggle.

on making the scene

her lover is also pleased with her performance. last night
Pus won an award   Most Improved Player for extended play
with Vixen who's very skilful. Vixen has many girls on the go.
Most Improved Player! this is what being young is all about.
experimentation   trust mixed with danger   smell of leather
stale perfume   whips of pleasure   words of pain
sweet really.

so lonely

sudden clap of thunder   sky changes colour   another storm
sheets of rain bed down the city into darkness.

getting old

Kat is homeless escaping the deluge huddled in a doorway.
Kat believes she is a cat   hair two-toned blonde-black
    little peaks where a cat's ears would be
wears lots of silver pieced ears   nose and lip
torn tartan frock   her T-shirt slogan SEX PISTOLS RULE
yellow-black striped leggings suggest a feral cat
a red lipstick heart is smeared on her cheek
travels with a friend   his dirty T-shirt bleeds YUPPIES SUK.
they've a little carrying case where two rats reside
the rats are called CUNT and SLUT
people can get quite upset when she's talking to her pets.

things might get better

splinters of rain attack the hospital windows
Julie fiddles with a radio
below   Pus is a lone figure bent against the wind
hoping for a lift   worrying *where's Vixen tonight?*
and *who's she with?*
behind the hospital Kat jumps oily puddles
sloshing her way to the Church-run soup kitchen.
Julie hears on the radio *weather forecast heavy rain
   easing to showers.*

she'll find out soon enough she's pregnant.

displaced

home is the most dangerous place for a woman to be. two women every week die from domestic violence in Australia. Aboriginal women are 34 times more likely to be hospitalised as a result of domestic violence than women in the rest of the community. city women have stopped closure of some women's refuges reversing the 'road home' funding changes but it's a different story regionally: 'listen up: as a well-known Christian charity we offer sanctuary for alcoholic drug-affected women or victims of domestic violence and their children in countless country areas and i'm proud to tell you we are open for business. though many of our beds are empty (this is the first time in thirty years) we're confident we'll gain your trust. unfortunately we had to let go all former staff who talked too freely with the media but we hold them closely in our prayers. safety is of prime importance. unstable and volatile mentally ill women will be heavily sedated. we don't provide staff overnight as before but believe locked doors will give sufficient security. authorities are only a phone call away. don't be concerned that child sexual abuse or the legacy of the stolen generation will be an issue because of our past history. it is our Christian duty to provide a place of safety for unhappy souls to rebuild their broken lives and quickly get safely on home.'

homeless

they cram into tents in Belmore Park.
a million dollars the cost of an average home in Sydney
billions to house asylum seekers offshore.

after the accident
slide down spiral of madness
to cardboard covered by a blanket
dog Bluey by her side. people say *get rid of the mutt.*
her only friend barks at danger   warns off strangers.
knife attack took eight dollars made her fear worse.
don't block the footpath   move on.

> in fifty large cities of the United States
> now a crime to feed street people
> directive from police officer: *drop that plate*
> Love Thy Neighbour   *stop feeding the poor*
> violations carry penalties – $500 fine or 60 days in jail.
> left with no food or coffee   homeless hungry people.

some people think it's god's punishment
destiny or choice
– *make your bed   you lie in it*

head lowered   wipes tears from his eyes
gnaws at his knuckles
homeless veteran of the Iraq war
did tour of duty with honour
came home with post-traumatic stress disorder.
just another derelict
wrapped in a blanket   on the street in Darlinghurst.

'light a candle for freedom raise your voice for justice'

Kavisha Mazzella & Marcia Howard, *Concert for East Timor*

ships of dreams

Australian mining billionaire Clive Palmer
plans to be the next prime minister of Australia
is cloning dinosaurs for a new Jurassic-style Disneyland?
has ordered instead an army of giant animatronic replicas
165 of them from China   20 feet tall and weighing a ton
he aims to rebuild the Titanic as a cinematic theme park
cruise on the ocean liner   costumes supplied
dancing in the ballroom   bejewelled ladies
in elegant frocks   gentlemen in Edwardian evening garb
code of chivalry lost on those who tweet today said Clive
chandeliers sparkle above a tuxedoed orchestra
no dead bodies in the bunks below
he's dreaming long into the future of a fleet
Titanic three and four built by Chinese hands
with his ore return of the ghost ship from the ocean floor
rich folks saved while down in steerage drowned the poor
we'll recreate 'em! a massive business opportunity!
pay a fortune for a first-class cabin on Titanic II
complete with four funnels   grand staircase
Turkish baths but with a casino   satellite navigation
and more lifeboats   *one of the benefits of global warming*
he said   *less icebergs*

earth art

wake to a blood-orange sky
winds of drought dump red dust
tons of topsoil blow on Sydney
outback dirt in every crack and cranny
someone mutters *climate change?*
suddenly we're on Mars! we take photos
sand-dunes climb windowsill geranium pots
our tracks   lost in dots…

red ochre   desert symbol   blood of ancestral beings
mix pigments on a palette   add bone feathers
charcoal   orchid sap   sparkles of radioactive dust
from Maralinga.   stencil in the Harbour Bridge
smudge tall buildings   Sydney Opera House
finger paint a wash of orange sails.
remove aircraft and harbour ferries
with the stroke of a crushed stick brush
covered in strands of human hair.

Chowder Bay   samples measure phytoplankton
ocean blooms   unique microscopic life
feeds on CO_2 a month's coal fired
power station emissions.

frontier wars

'next out of our kitchen taps comes water on fire.'
Nanna Joan's knitted yellow hat bobs.
'nowhere is sacred. fracking fluids
    cause hazardous water contamination.
vast fluctuations in groundwater levels. in the air
    fugitive emissions known to be carcinogenic
have unknown effect on the environment   on health.'
she reaches for another ball of buttercup yellow wool.
    NO GAS sign flutters at a Gloucester
KNITTING NANNAS AGAINST GAS demo.

Nanna Mavis's needles click release a stream of honey
her long golden scarf to toss across a bulldozer.
'in summer the Worimi hunted here   fished
winter the tribes went inland. flora   fauna thrived.
the land was replenished. balance restored.
then came cedar-cutters with bullocks and blades
logged the trees. cattle grazed on sacred sites
water holes were poisoned   wildlife vanished.'

Nan Skye nods as she knits daffodil and black squares
'settlers gave Aborigines gifts of food
laced with arsenic. fast forward   people are sick
coal seam gas licences or applications
cover more than half the country
    including traditional lands. the banks
mining companies   force farmers out. it's legal theft.
we're flogging off the family farm overseas.
abandoned homesteads   prime agricultural estates
are quarries   alien industrial moonscapes.'

'knit sister knit' says Kate 'we're knitting a
revolution. the gas project is shut down for now.
CEO resigned. it's in the local paper. read all about it:
buy-backs and cancellations of CSG licences.
with cost of production *higher* than the *price* of gas
funds cut to research energy from natural sources.
NSW government *approves* a billion tonnes of new coal.
yay!' Nanna Mack exclaims,
'you sound like headlines in the *Advocate*.'
signs flap: SHUT THE GATE
    FRACK FREE ZONE.
'elevated toxic BTEX levels in the wells.
how did it get like this? they should monitor
the industry more closely.'

'Mack' soothes Nanna Joan 'we *are* winning
against the gas company wrecking
our beautiful valley.' more signs at feet of the Nannas:
YOU CANT EAT COAL CANT DRINK GAS
    THE FUTURE IS RENEWABLE.
Nanna Mavis pipes up 'they're still licensed
to explore for more. we say leave it in the ground
for the sake of the kiddies.'
Joan mumbles 'remember when AGL
gave out hats and balloons at the show
children became walking advertisements.'
Nan Skye sighs 'we all feel the heat of climate change.
heard that the Galilee Basin is a huge carbon bomb.
Barrier Reef is under threat
with the passage of coal and gas exports.
if water quality fails   the reef dies.'

their complaints grow woven together
    strand by strand.
'even Dorothea Mackellar's Kurrumbede was sold
    for coal mining. 'My Country'   don't think so   dear.
finished – another woolly jumper
        for a penguin injured in an oil spill.'

rain

a poet wakes early to catch the muse and shuffles to find pen and paper as rain patter-pings the frangipani. city workers feet thud drumming pavements to jobs they hope will still be there. under blue skies a grazier walks his pasture's red dust. kicks the cracked mud in the dry dam. he reaches for his rifle. first the grazier shoots the cattle. a solitary bird flies above white bones exposed in drought burnt paddocks. the grazier fires a final shot and falls. stillness. the poet crawls inside a page that suddenly ignites and bursts into flame. inked squiggles disintegrate into blackened ash. buildings in the city obscure the sky. the sudden flight of birds. caught on a fence-post native grasses wriggle free. city workers rush back from jobs that pay for cars in parking stations. empty mortgaged houses that wait a nightly dark returning. defiant. in her own world despite storms of doubt the poet reaches for a pen. paper. and turns another page. words rain down. the breath rises and falls.

global warning

past brightly lit shops
vast car sale-yards
ice-cold air-conditioned bus
hurtles along
a young woman   sniffs and sniffs
blows gusts of germs into hanky
out steamy windows
a deluge of pelting rain
uneasy passengers slip side to side
fish on deck
they slither and slide

deep furrows of ploughed worries
man frowning
glares at his crossword
Down   somebody or something
foreshadows a future event (9)
h a r b i n g e r
downpours
drowned islands

Down   another word to flood
place with water (8)
i n u n d a t e
blocked drains   flooded roads
an elderly woman on fast tippy-toes
slippery on wet floor
skates to the back of the bus

driver turns up his radio to hear
sliver of ice bridging Wilkins Ice Shelf
wrenching away from Antarctic Peninsular
(the size of Jamaica)
collapsed exploding into hundreds of floating icebergs

Across method of identification (12)
f i n g e r p r i n t s
warming poles
melting glaciers rising sea levels
woman rubs her bruised ankle
sudden rush of water swirls against the bus window
she ponders the future

Down   marks the end of the world
his tongue protrudes as the man pencils
a final and decisive war or <u>conflict</u> (10)
A r m a g e d d o n
Antarctic ice melts
Sydney disappears underwater

bear that is not

a koala is asleep in the eucalypt tree-fork
high above my squinting self
in the sunset   darkening
        outside our cabin by the Myall shores
waders stand all leggy at the water's edge
the ferryman waits for coin.

koalas breed only once a year   blind hairless joeys
crawl into her pouch when about an inch long.
fossils found of some kind of koala
date back twenty-five million years.
a bear that is not a bear.

we passed Myall Lakes as a kid with my family
crossed to Tuncurry from Forster by car ferry
when travelling up north for Christmas.
we did not stop for scenery   to look at birds
koalas   wombats   or kangaroos.

the koala stares down at me
before shifting her weight   falling back to sleep.
in the bluegreen sea over the sand dunes
a pod of svelte dolphins surf the waves
a whale further out is breaching   tail smacking the sea.

i hear barking. is the koala protecting territorial rights
        or mourning their destruction?
hazy memories of bushfire devastation
chance survival when hunted as food or fur
evading the fangs of wild dogs snarling?

is the koala hallucinating:
unstoppable deliberately introduced cane toads
jumping across Kakadu that keep breeding
with no natural predators.
lamenting honeybees wiped out by pesticides
        or something else…
worker bees staging a spring offensive
a lost revolutionary uprising against the queen
turning the sky black?

is the nightmare of a whitened carcass
the Great Barrier Reef
smothered in toxic dredge spoil
with all the luminous fish vanished
in the too warm rising of the sea
scary enough for a koala
to seek escape in blissful arboreal safety?

koala habitat is logged for roads
to six-bedroom five-bathroom mansions
with more roads for timber trucks
open-cut coalmines in forests
fracking coal seam gas leaking methane
in polluted water   ecological disasters.

without a plan our natural world   tree-snuggled koalas
all the beauty's feathered whirr iridescence
wild bird calling   is silenced and departed forever.

borderlines

1.

with wars come refugees
forty-three West Papuan men women and children
five weeks in wild seas in a traditional double outrigger
        canoe drifting four days without food or water
washed ashore on Queensland's Cape York Peninsula
relocated to Christmas Island – *if sent back we will die*
one of many who served prison time
   for raising outlawed flag
pro-independence activists for decades
   are hunted in the jungle a slow genocide:
   raped imprisoned tortured shot
bodies thrown in the river houses burnt land occupied
boys from the remote highlands sent alone to the sea

while at the north-west point on Christmas Island
construction cranes swoop across a new detention centre
another prison for those fleeing persecution

2.

out-of-control bushfires burn red across the skyline
cricket bats *thwack* tennis balls *pock*
in scorching summer heat frolic in a pool
dive in the ocean who cares about refugees?

climate change is absolute crap says Tony Abbott
evacuees from drowned islands
homes swallowed by the sea
are economic migrants we deliver straight to PNG

the Australian navy tows asylum boats back
cuts them loose in Indonesian waters
saves refugees from drowning
surrendering then to suicidal despair

seeking asylum is a human right
our colonial plan is to dump 'em overseas
fails to meet international standards
> UN found conditions on Manus Island
> *harsh   hot   humid   damp   and cramped.*

3.

next we must stop the birds
crossing sovereign borders
send them packing
process them in cages offshore
as the European pigeon said to an Indian mynah:
go back where you came from.

Under Canvas

From the director of *Stop the Boats!* comes *Under Canvas* that has the critics talking with the ficto-factual thriller revealing layers of misery in harsh light of a tent city's hunger-strikes riots hangings throat-slittings and a murder. Flashbacks intersect a boat trip across perilous waters to a war zone's bombed-out city torture and rapes. Horrific repetitions of violent imagery such as close ups of lips sewn with black thread compel you to look away. An aerial shot pans over a tiny island and abandoned phosphate mine. Drenching rain and rough seas. Close up to an orange witch's hat on the tarmac that says Air Nauru. A young girl disembarks alone. She is a transferee sent to a remote detention centre with army-style tents and no air-conditioning humid and dusty. As she steps onto the steaming tarmac a guitar licks Woody Guthrie's *and all they will call you will be deportees*. The girl with no name is superbly played by the young Iranian actress Anahita Farahani who displays great dignity when authorities inform her she's to be relocated again this time to Cambodia. Chronic diseases threaten two hundred other kids who cough and cry or stare blankly to camera. A trio of oud double bass and a hand drum's measured beat is astonishingly ominous. The sounds of waves and men arguing. The power is off and water scarce. Shadows lengthen. Shafts of torchlight dancing. In a slow tracking shot a child is sexually assaulted on a lengthy walk to the toilet block. Brutal. Disappointing is the lack of subtlety in the film *Under Canvas* where detainees' paranoia and loss of innocence are contrasted with the undercurrent of violence and injustice. With projected sequel from Manus Island expected next summer you wonder where will we be taken next. *Pirates of the Indian Ocean* as Tamil asylum seekers trapped in isolation for a month on board customs vessel are threatened with forcible return to India by lifeboat. *No Safe Haven for You Here?*

razor wire

number 82176 is two no toys
adults make kites
coloured rubbish bags
guards confiscate them
number 82176 is in tears

plays with garbage
wailing waddling
little hands waving

ahead of UN inspection
detainees are to be referred to by name not number
have their rooms repainted trees planted
razor wire removed

red dust swirls heat no fans
Fatimah (number 82176) stays locked away
        indefinitely

composition of suffering

the news photo could win awards
beautifully framed   two Rohingya youths
wet and exhausted   bedraggled young bodies
passed out or dead.
a policeman reaches in to lend a hand
an Indonesian soldier covers his ears
another man with cap and jeans   just stares

shunned gypsies of Asia
survivors from a rickety vessel
in sarongs and singlets
backs scarred from beatings
refugees or immigrants
towed out to sea
without an engine
drifted for three weeks
running out of food and water

they couldn't swim if they should fall
no room to sit they stood for twenty-one days

light shimmers over shadows
sweat glistens   they gasp
lens closes on a prize-winning portrait

grief-stricken

(meaning of Malala in Urdu)

schoolgirls giggle in the van
taking us home
to the Swat valley
a masked man
pushes his way
down the aisle   *Malala?*
    which of you is Malala?
wish I'd said
  we are all Malala
but didn't.

the Taliban gunman
shot her in the head
    fifteen years old
the noise   deafening
I thought she was dead.

Taliban banned girls
going to school   watching TV
listening to music
shopping with our mothers.
they bombed girls' schools
left death threats.

Taliban said she was an American spy.
ten men were tried   found guilty
but secretly   eight were released
the man that pulled the trigger   vanished.

she cannot come home
youngest ever awarded
the Nobel Peace Prize
is still funny
teases her brothers
her face
        frozen
    down one side.

the Taliban
picked the wrong girl
gave fire to her courage
she wanted to be a teacher
now   politician.

she's the voice for girls
everywhere.
our right to education
become grown women
free from violence
independent and equal.

> *one book*
> *one pen*
> *one child*
> *one teacher*
> *can change the world*
>   – Malala Yousafzai

Sydney Siege

in the heart of the city
hours pass slowly   TV cameras shoot
hostages with hands against the windows
at the Lindt Chocolat Café in Martin Place.

he was a man of peace   he said
carried a prayer banner and shotgun
pen is my gun   words are my bullets
claimed there was a bomb in his backpack.

rapid flashes of police gunfire
red ribbons among tinsel and cellophane
chocolates wrapped for Christmas
peppered with bullets.

sprinkles of rain lightly fell
on field of flowers left by mourners
that became a shrine
with a plaque for the dead.

snarled in traffic
the city is open for business
thousands offer *#illridewithyou*
        for those fearing racist backlash
yet women in headscarves are spat on.

'ah, but in such an ugly time the true protest is beauty'

Phil Ochs

into blue

space junk has in cracks and crannies life forms that change with intense heat into a subatomic new life force that melds with a meteorite on re-entry merges with everything metallic on Earth to form a new cosmic collective consciousness that's galaxy-blue and humming. they've come home to their Creators. first law of hummers is to harm no humans. fridges phones buildings home billion-dollar aircraft and bombs are turning blue and hum. guns and bullets purr in people's pockets. a young thug at a convenience store pulls a knife that squeals turns blue is hot and rubbery. with a yelp of pain the youth flees. the knife returns to a pleasant vibrating whirr. in war zones planes with bluish bombs refuse to fly. rockets won't fire. cars don't crash. galaxy-blue is hard for dye makers to match but soon the populace of New York and London are kitted out in blue. some begin to worship hummers as the new manifestation of Krishna. first were hip-replacements but now bodies turn blue as Avatars in the fantasy film. no more wars. we hold our breath. turn galaxy-blue. – awake breathless hear on the radio David Bowie singing *Planet Earth is blue. And there's nothing I can do…* a blue marble spinning in the cosmic playground is in danger of losing the game.

www.ingramcontent.com/pod-product-compliance
Lightning Source LLC
Chambersburg PA
CBHW062142100526
44589CB00014B/1664